Joe Schuster

ONE SEASON
IN THE SUN

Joe Schuster teaches at Webster University.
His novel *The Might Have Been* was published
in 2012. His short fiction has appeared in
The Kenyon Review, *The Iowa Review*, and *The
Missouri Review*, among others, and his articles
have been published in *USA Today*, *St. Louis
Post-Dispatch* and the revered, retired *Sport*.

First published by GemmaMedia in 2012.

GemmaMedia
230 Commercial Street
Boston, MA 02109 USA

www.gemmamedia.com

Printed in the United States of America

16   15   14   8   9

978-1-936846-22-1

Library of Congress Cataloging-in-Publication Data

Schuster, Joseph M.
One season in the sun / Joe Schuster.
   p. cm. — (Open door)
ISBN 978-1-936846-22-1 (pbk.)
1. Baseball—United States. 2. Baseball players—United
States. 3. Buehrle, Mark. 4. Wise, DeWayne. I. Title.
GV863.A1.S38 2012
796.357—dc23

                                        012027683

Cover by Night & Day Design

Inspired by the Irish series of books designed for adult literacy, Gemma Open Door Foundation provides fresh stories, new ideas, and essential resources for young people and adults as they embrace the power of reading and the written word.

Brian Bouldrey
North American Series Editor

GEMMA
Open Door

For Kathy and all my family,
devoted baseball fans.

ONE

Three Innings and Gone

In 1964, when Dave Bakenhaster was nineteen years old, his life seemed like a story from a movie.

When he was eight, he became an orphan. Both his mother and father died within six months of each other. Bakenhaster went to live with one of his older brothers. He dealt with his grief by devoting himself to baseball. The boy promised his family that he would one day be good enough at the sport people called "America's pastime" to play in the major leagues. By high school, he was one of the best teenage pitchers in the country. Over four years, he won forty games and lost only four. In his last two seasons, he struck out 461 batters in just 214 innings, a phenomenal number in itself. He threw nine no-hit games, and in one, struck out every batter he faced.

With such success, it is not surprising that when he graduated, almost every major league team joined a bidding war to convince him to pitch for them. The highest bidder was St. Louis. The Cardinals paid him roughly $40,000 just to sign a contract.

Although the amount seems small compared with the million-dollar-plus bonuses that talented ballplayers can earn now on signing, $40,000 was a large sum in the early 1960s. It was almost eight times what an average American worker earned for an entire year. You could buy a new two-bedroom home in a St. Louis suburb for $8,500 or a luxury three-bedroom home on a golf course for $20,000. A new Dodge sedan carried a price sticker of $1,800. Gasoline cost less than thirty cents a gallon.

Bakenhaster's signing was so big that newspapers across the county published stories about the deal.

The next year, not even legally old enough to vote or drink, he reached the goal he'd set not long after his parents died: Dave Bakenhaster was in the major leagues. On a hot and muggy late June afternoon in St. Louis, with more than 20,000 fans watching, he made his debut against the San Francisco Giants.

The Giants' team was powerful. Five of its members—Willie Mays, Orlando

Cepeda, Duke Snider, Gaylord Perry and Juan Marichal—would one day end up in baseball's Hall of Fame, the museum that honors the best baseball players in the game's history. By the time Bakenhaster took the mound in the eighth inning, the Giants were already leading 10–1.

The first batter he faced hit a double, but Bakenhaster got the next two men to ground out. The fourth hitter was Willie Mays, one of the greatest baseball players in the history of the game. Bakenhaster threw a pitch that Mays hit on the ground to the shortstop. That should have been the last out of the inning, but the shortstop made an error and Mays was safe. The other runner scored. The Giants followed with two more singles, tallying two more runs, before Bakenaster finally retired them. He allowed one more run in the ninth inning.

A month later against the Pittsburgh Pirates, Bakenhaster appeared in his second game. He pitched an inning in another lop-sided loss and allowed two runs and three hits.

The next day, the Hollywood story ended.

The Cardinals sent him back to the minor leagues. Perhaps because he was disappointed that he had little chance in the major leagues, he pitched poorly for the rest of the year. He won only one game, lost six, and allowed more than five runs every time he was on the mound.

He did not play well in the next minor league season, but 1966, when he was a twenty-year-old in the class A Florida State League, he pitched as the professional scouts had expected he would. He finished the year with more victories than all but one other pitcher in the league and was among the league leaders in most other pitching categories.

It was not enough to help him get back to the major leagues. The Cardinals had other pitchers they were more interested in bringing along, like future Hall of Fame member Steve Carlton and future All Star Jerry Reuss.

Bakenhaster spent three more years in the minor leagues and then decided to retire as a player. The Cardinals offered him a job as a coach for the next year and he accepted. Less than a week after he agreed, however, he told the team he had changed his mind, citing "personal reasons."

Dave Bakenhaster walked away from the game, at the young age of twenty-five, and went to work in a warehouse near the Ohio home where he'd grown up.

TWO

Loving Baseball

When I was a boy, I wanted to be Dave Bakenhaster. I don't mean I wanted to be him, specifically, but someone like him. I was eleven the summer he spent his brief moment in the major leagues, and I imagined myself some years into my future playing baseball for the St. Louis Cardinals, my favorite team. On most nights throughout the spring and summer, I listened to their games on a transistor radio hidden under my pillow. I kept the volume low so my parents would not know I was tuned in when I was supposed to be sleeping.

I knew the names of the players in the

starting lineup: Lou Brock, Bill White, Curt Flood, Julian Javier, and the others. My brother and I played wiffle ball in our backyard, alternating as pitcher and hitter. When I batted, I pretended to be one of the starting Cardinals, announcing to my brother who I imagined myself each time.

Every week, my parents gave me an allowance of twenty-five cents. As soon as I had the money, I walked to a drug store near our house and spent it all on Topps baseball cards. A package cost a nickel and contained five cards and a stick of pink gum coated in fine, white, powdered sugar. Each card had the glossy color photograph of a major league player on one side and, on the other, his batting or pitching statistics. At first, I kept the cards stacked in a shoebox. As I collected more and more, the shoebox became too small to hold them all. Then I stored them in a Styrofoam ice chest.

I spent hours reading those cards, the players' numbers of home runs and strikeouts. I loved baseball so much, in fact, that my father taught me how to calculate percentages by showing me the formula for a player's batting average: take the number of his base hits and divide it by the number of times he batted. Twenty-five hits in 100 at bats meant a .250 batting average. Thirty hits in 100 at bats meant a .300 batting average. I learned that even such a small difference in hits meant one player was great and another merely good. Or less than good. A player with a .300 batting average was great. A player with a .250 average was not. Subtract even a few more hits for every 100 times a player batted and he was fair or even poor.

One night, I read through twenty or thirty cards, doing the math, checking to see if the statisticians at Topps had made errors in their calculations. They had not.

While I coveted the baseball cards of the stars in the game then, the players who would eventually be in the Hall of Fame at Cooperstown, New York—Willie Mays, Mickey Mantle, Bob Gibson, Carl Yastrzemski, Sandy Koufax, Harmon Killebrew—the players who most intrigued me were the marginal ones. I was interested in the players who would never be in the Hall of Fame or earn a place on an All Star team.

In 1964, The Topps Baseball Card Company produced 587 different baseball cards, numbering each in a tiny image of a baseball on the back in the upper left corner. The company honored the best players by giving them numbers ending in a zero. Number 50 was Mickey Mantle, who had been a member of his League's All Star team in all twelve of the previous years. Willie Mays, an All Star for ten years, was card 150. Sandy Koufax, who was such a great left-handed pitcher his nickname was "The Left Hand of God," appeared on card 200.

The players who were not yet the stars (and who might never be stars) were shown on cards with numbers you couldn't divide by ten. Bakenhaster was on card 479. Another player appears on card 561. Dave Bennett's major league career was even shorter than Bakenhaster's—one inning. Steve Hertz, who had no hits in the five times he batted in the major leagues, was on card 544.

These were the players who fascinated me. The stars—Mays, Mantle, Koufax—all seemed beyond human, blessed by a divine miracle. The others, who never made an All Star team, who seemed to spend more time sitting on a bench during games than on the field, who lasted in the major leagues for only days or weeks—they seemed more like ordinary men whose bit of luck earned them a major league uniform.

They were, I thought as I looked at their cards, more akin to me. As much as

I loved baseball, as much as I spent hours memorizing the information on the backs of baseball cards and reading the statistics that the Sunday newspaper published in the sports section, as much as I learned the history of the game, I couldn't play it. I was heavy, slow, and myopic.

A few years after the season when Bakenhaster, Bennett, and Hertz all had their brief time in the major leagues, I would try out for the team at my high school. Because I couldn't run and couldn't hit, I decided I was a pitcher. But, on the first day of practice, when the coach gave me a chance to show him my ability on the mound, I couldn't throw a strike. Every pitch was what they call a lollipop—a slow, high-arching throw to the catcher. The next day, when the coach posted the names of the players he was cutting after only a single practice, my name was on the list with one other boy. I have since come to see that the coach saved both of us time. No matter how much he loved the game, there is no point in a boy who can't play at all taking time away from the boys who were faster, who could throw the ball with speed and accuracy, who could hit the ball to the deepest part of the field.

That afternoon, however, seeing my name on the sheet of paper tacked to a bulletin board in the school hallway, telling me I couldn't play and would most likely never be good enough to play, I was heartbroken.

THREE

A Difficult Line to Cross

While I might have imagined I was like the men who reached the major leagues but could not last more than a few weeks, the truth is, I was nothing like them on the field. Bakenhaster and others may have spent less than an hour of their lives playing in a big league uniform, unlike other men who played for ten or even twenty seasons. Still, they were extraordinary.

For most of the regular baseball season, there are only 750 major league players at any one point. (In September, once the minor league season ends, teams may add more players to their rosters.) To give you an idea of how small that number is, consider that in October 2011, Apple, which had more than 50,000 employees in total, had 1,000 computer engineers working on the company's project to design and develop new computer chips.

There were 250 more computer engineers at one company working on a single project than there are major league players across all of the thirty teams.

When Dave Bakenhaster had his moment in the sun, big league jobs were even scarcer. There were only twenty teams then, meaning there were only 500 major league spots that summer. Before 1961, there were even fewer, because there were only sixteen major league teams.

It is no surprise that getting to the major leagues for even a single time at the plate or a single inning as a pitcher is a rare thing indeed.

How rare?

Consider a high school ballplayer good enough to be a member of his varsity team. He's already proven he's among the best in his community, his city, or his state. But he is still a long shot to push his way to the top of the sport.

I read somewhere that only one of every ninety-four baseball players who puts on a high school uniform will end up playing for a professional team, even at the lowest level of the minor leagues.

Once in the minors—among the top one and a half percent of baseball talent in the country—players still face significant odds against ever playing in the majors. *Baseball America* estimates that of all minor league players, only ten percent will get into a single game in the majors. From the original number of good high school players, then, just slightly more than one out of every thousand will step onto a major league field for even a single minute of a game.

(In case you wondered, there have been roughly 18,000 major league players in the history of the sport. To put the odds into perspective, in more than 140 years since the beginning of professional baseball, less than forty percent of the number of people working for Apple in October, 2011 have been able to call themselves major league players.)

How difficult is it to push through the wall that separates the minor leagues from the majors?

One way to understand this is to look at the results of the annual draft the major league teams hold. Every June, organizations take turns to select the high school or college ballplayers they want to add to their rosters. In recent years, the draft has had fifty rounds as teams choose the players they believe have the best talent early on.

Often, the scouts are correct in the choices they make. In 2001, for example, the Minnesota Twins chose a catcher named Joe Mauer with the first pick in the draft. He reached the major leagues in 2004 after three years in the minors. By 2005, he was the Twins' starting catcher, and in four seasons after that, he made the league All Star team. In 2009, baseball writers named him the

Most Valuable Player in the American League.

But sometimes, the scouts are wrong. In 2002, the Cincinnati Reds paid high school pitcher Chris Gruler $2.5 million just to sign a contract as their top pick in the annual draft. He was the third player any team chose that year, out of almost 1,500 players over fifty rounds of the draft. With their choice, the Reds were saying that they thought that Gruler was the third best among all the players. Despite their faith, he never reached the major leagues.

Because of arm injuries, he appeared in only twenty-seven games in the low minor leagues. After five years, the Reds let him go. He was twenty-two, and his baseball career was finished.

That same year, the Montreal Expos gave a similar bonus to pitcher Clint Everts, their top pick in the draft. Unlike Gruler, Everts continued pitching in the minor leagues. In nine seasons through 2011, he appeared in almost 300 games and was still waiting for his chance for the major leagues.

Out of the 2002 draft, six of the thirty players chosen in the first round have never appeared in the major leagues. In the 2001 draft, ten of the thirty first-round players never reached the majors, although at the time, they were considered the best of the best.

It is tempting, maybe, to think of Dave Bakenhaster (and nearly 4,000 players who lasted a season or less in their major league careers) as a failure in the sport. He got to the top, but he couldn't stick. But in the context of Gruler and Everts and the other ninety percent of professional ballplayers who never did—or haven't yet—reached the major leagues, Bakenhaster and his 4,000 fellow players who had only one season in the sun seem like successes.

FOUR

Why They Can't Stick

We do face a question, however.

If one-season players are good enough to reach the major leagues, why don't they last longer than the one at bat, the one game, the one week, one month, or one year?

Four men suffered tragic ends to their careers. They died during their one-and-only season in the major leagues or immediately after it.

Pitcher Frank Leary, who was in two games for the Cincinnati Reds in 1907, succumbed after surgery to remove his appendix in October of the same year. Charlie Peete, who appeared in twenty-three games for the 1956 St. Louis Cardinals, perished in a plane crash on his way to play baseball in Venezuela during the winter after the season finished. Pitcher Dick Wantz appeared in one game for the California Angels in April 1965 and struck out two batters in one inning while allowing two runs. When he left the mound, he said he had a severe headache. It turned out to be an inoperable brain tumor, and he died a month later. Cincinnati Reds' outfielder Dernell Stensen appeared in thirty-seven games in 2003. When the season was over, the Reds sent him to play in a fall league in Arizona to sharpen his skills. Tragically, he was murdered in November in what police suspect was a carjacking.

Two other players died in combat during World War II a few years after their single season in the major leagues. Harry O'Neill, who appeared as a catcher for the Philadelphia Athletics in only a single inning in 1939, joined the Marines a few months after the Japanese attacked the Pearl Harbor Naval Base in December 1941. He died in March 1945 in the battle for Iwo Jima.

Elmer Gedeon played in five games for the Washington Senators, also in 1939. In one of those games, Gedeon was great. He had three hits in four times at bat and made what *The New York Times* called a "beautiful running catch." He joined the Army one month after the Pearl Harbor attack and became a bomber pilot. In 1943, he earned a medal for heroism when he saved a member of his crew after their plane crashed. The next year, Gedeon died when German artillery shot down his plane over France.

O'Neill and Gedeon were the only two players with major league experience who died in combat during the war.

Many men suffered injuries that ended their short baseball careers. John Paciorak, one of three brothers who played in the major leagues, appeared in one big league game. In 1963, he was eighteen, and his team, the Houston Colt 45s (now the Astros) decided to start a lineup of all rookie players on the season's last day as a publicity stunt. Paciorak played right field and had a perfect day at the plate. He came up five times, walked twice, and made three hits. Then he hurt his back, and for the next six years, the injury plagued him. He missed one entire year because of his health and saw an average of only fifty-six games in the other seasons. Finally, at the age of twenty-four, he was finished.

Pitcher Larry Yount had even worse luck than Pacioarak.

In 1971, he was twenty-one, and the Astros added him to their roster in September. On the fifteenth, he took the mound as a relief pitcher to start the ninth inning. Before facing a batter, most pitchers take eight warm-up throws to the catcher so that their arm is loose. On Yount's second warm-up pitch, he injured his elbow and had to leave the game without ever throwing an official pitch. Because he'd been announced as being in the game, his name remained in the box score. He went back to the minor leagues the next season, and four years later his career ended without a return to the major leagues. He is the only pitcher in history to have a record of appearing in a game without ever actually throwing the ball to a batter.

(Like Paciorak, Yount had a brother who played in the major leagues. He is Robin Yount, who is honored in the Baseball Hall of Fame.)

Some guys had the bad fortune of playing in the wrong organization. Outfielder Carl Boles, whose major league career consisted of nineteen games in 1962, gave evidence he was good enough to last longer. In his twenty-four at bats, he had nine hits for a robust

.375 batting average. But Boles played for a team that had an outfield headed for the Hall of Fame—Willie Mays and Willie McCovey—as well as one of the best hitters of the era. Felipe Alou, was also a member the National League All Star team that year. Boles eventually left the U.S. to play baseball in Japan, where he ranked among the best home run hitters in his league in two seasons and made two All Star teams.

Some players just walked away. In 1903, Henry Schmidt was one of the best pitchers in baseball. Then twenty-two, he was pitching for Brooklyn and won twenty-two games, more than all but four other pitchers in the National League. He was from California, however, and when Brooklyn sent him a contract for the next year, he returned it unsigned. He sent a note saying he preferred living on the west coast. He spent five more seasons pitching in the minor leagues, and then left the game altogether.

Most of the men, however, didn't last because they apparently were not equal to the superior level of play in the majors. About half of the 1,800 non-pitchers who spent a year or less in the major leagues batted .220 or lower during their brief stay. Still, many of them ranked among the top hitters in the minor leagues during some of their seasons there.

Almost a thousand appeared in only one game. About 125 of the players who were not pitchers had the chance to bat only once. Another seventy spent years in the minor leagues, got to the major leagues but never had the chance to bat at all.

Out of the more than 500 pitchers who got into only one game, 150 pitched an inning or less.

Still, some of them knew a moment of glory and saw their names in the headlines in the sports pages before they slipped back into the fog of obscurity, descending to the minor leagues or back to the world that was life outside baseball. They hit dramatic home runs in extra innings to win ball games. They threw shutouts.

They're part of the history of America's pastime and deserve our notice of their single seasons in the sun.

FIVE

Pioneers

For some players, the obstacles that kept them out of the major leagues, or shortened their time if they did, had little to do with talent.

They had everything to do with race.

For half a century, the major leagues refused to allow African-Americans to play baseball for any of their teams, including the minor league outfits.

As well as baseball historians can tell, the first African-American player to wear a major league uniform was William Edward White, who played one game when he was nineteen years old for the

Providence (Rhode Island) Grays on June 21, 1879. He had a base hit in four at bats and then left baseball; historians say he moved to Chicago and became a bookkeeper.

Five years later, in 1884, another African-American player named Moses Fleetwood Walker appeared in forty-two games for Toledo (then a major league team.) His brother, Welday Walker, also played five games for the same team that year. Because he was African-American, Moses Walker faced extreme bias on the field, even from his own teammates. Hall of Fame player and manager Cap Anson said openly, more than once, that he would refuse to play a game if Moses Walker were on the same field. A few years later, that prejudice caused baseball owners to vote to ban African-American players from the professional game.

That ban stood until 1946, when the Brooklyn Dodgers signed a player named Jackie Robinson to a contract. After one season in the minor leagues, Robinson made it to the majors in 1947. He helped the Dodgers reach the World Series that season and played for ten years. After he retired, he was elected to Baseball's Hall of Fame.

When he reached the major leagues, Robinson was already twenty-eight, a relatively older age for someone to start a major league career. With his talent, he most likely would have been in the major leagues several years earlier, if bias hadn't kept him out. But, in truth, he was luckier than many other African-

American baseball players who never had a chance to play major league baseball. He fared better than those who did play but reached the major leagues several years after their skills had started to decline and so could only play for a short time.

If we look only at what James "Bus" Clarkson did in the major leagues, we might decide that he was not a good ballplayer. In 1952, when he was thirty-seven years old, he got into fourteen games with the Boston Braves. He only had five hits in twenty-five at bats, and then the Braves let him go.

But when Clarkson was a younger man, he was a star in Negro league baseball.

Before 1947, the best African-American ballplayers played in what people called the "Negro National League" and the "Negro American League." Those leagues had organizations similar to major league baseball. Many of the most famous African-American stars in major league baseball during the 1950s started their professional careers in the Negro leagues. Aside from Jackie Robinson, other Hall of Fame major league players who started there were Henry Aaron, Ernie Banks, Larry Doby, and Willie Mays.

But Aaron, Mays, Doby, and Banks benefited from being younger than Clarkson when baseball lowered the wall that kept players of color out. Aaron, Mays, Doby, and Banks had not yet reached their prime when baseball abolished its shameful rule. In 1947, the best years of their lives as ballplayers were in front of them. That was not so for players like Clarkson, who often ranked among the ten best batters in the seasons he played Negro league baseball and when he appeared in the minor leagues before and after his short, fourteen-game major league career.

Without the ban, or if Clarkson had been younger than thirty-eight when it ended, he likely would have had a career that lasted longer than only part of one season.

Like Clarkson, Willard Brown only managed to play a few games in the major leagues. In his case, it was for the St. Louis Browns in 1947, when he was thirty-two. He made his debut three months after Jackie Robinson "broke the color barrier," but Brown only lasted for twenty-one games in the major leagues. He batted sixty-seven times and had twelve hits and one home run before the Browns released him. His batting average (.179) was even lower than Clarkson's. Like Clarkson, however, Brown was a great ballplayer who just happened to live most of his life during a time when he wasn't allowed in the major leagues. In eight seasons from the late 1930s to the late 1940s, he was one of the best hitters in the Negro Leagues. In two seasons, he had the highest batting average in the Negro American League; in three seasons, his batting average was the second best.

Brown did have two moments of glory in his short time in the major leagues.

In his fifth game, in late July against the New York Yankees, Brown batted five times, had four hits, and scored three runs. Three weeks later, he hit a home run to help his team win a game against the Detroit Tigers. He was the first African-American player to hit a home run for an American League team.

Brown's performance in that first game was so remarkable that the *New York Times* made note of it in their article about the game. But even in the newspaper's praise, we can see evidence that the bias that kept players out of baseball was still powerful.

The reporter wrote, "Leading the

thirteen-hit assault against Yankee [pitching] was sprightly Willard Brown, one of the two Negro players acquired recently by the Browns."

In its article about the game when he hit a home run, the *Times* again called him a "Negro player."

Over and over in sports articles in the late 1940s and early 1950s, when the idea that African-American players would appear on a major league field was still new, writers reminded their readers that the players were Negro. Columnists argued whether Negro players were actually good enough to belong in the major leagues.

That degree of racial bias meant that even in 1956, the tenth season after Jackie Robinson broke the baseball color barrier, there were few African-American players in the major leagues. Sixteen teams had only thirty-eight African-American players in total. Three teams had none; five teams had one.

Because the "color line" had kept African-American players out of baseball for so long, I have to wonder if others among the early African-American major leaguers might have had more than one season to shine.

Years after Willard Brown's brief career in the major leagues, he received a special honor.

In 2006, recognizing the wrong that baseball had done to African-American players for so much of the game's history, the Hall of Fame held a special election to recognize the greatest players in the history of the old Negro leagues. Voters chose twelve to induct into the Hall. One of them was Willard Brown. He was the only one of the dozen who had ever even played for a moment in the major leagues.

Sadly, Brown never knew. He died ten years before the vote.

SIX

Moments of Heroics on the Field

While it might seem that the story of every player who had just one season in the sun is nothing but sadness and disappointment, it's a fact that some had moments of triumph. They had game-winning hits that caused fans in the bleachers to leap to their feet, cheering. They had games that made them the best or one of the best major league players on any particular day.

Look at Bucky Jacobsen, for example.

Before he reached the major leagues, Jacobsen spent seven and a half seasons in the minor leagues, playing for teams in small and mid-sized towns like Ogden,

Utah, and Beloit, Wisconsin. In his second year in the minors, he hit the most home runs in his league and had the most runs batted in (RBI). In his fifth year, he again led his league in home runs and had the second most RBI.

Despite his success, he had trouble pushing past the final wall between the minor leagues and the majors. Part of his trouble was his main position at first base. In his first organization, the Milwaukee Brewers, the major league first baseman was a player named Richie Sexson. In three seasons, Sexson won the Gold Glove, the award major league baseball gives to the best fielder at each position. Sexson was also among the top home run hitters in the league.

After five years, Jacobsen moved from

the Brewers to the St. Louis Cardinals. Again, he led his league in home runs. But no matter how well he played in the minor leagues, he had little chance to be the everyday first baseman with the Cardinals. Their starting player at the position was Albert Pujols, a player many considered the best of his generation.

In 2004, after a year with the Cardinals, Jacobsen moved again, to the Seattle Mariners whose starting first baseman was near the end of his career. Jacobsen began the season in triple-A, the highest level of the minor leagues, and played so well that he won a place on the All Star team. The Mariners finally gave him his chance at the majors.

In his first big league game on July 16, he started hitting major league pitching as if he were a veteran and not a rookie. He had a base hit in that first game and in the second had two hits, including a home run. In his third game, he had two more hits and made his second home run. In his first ten games, he had ten hits, four of them home runs. After all of his years in the minor leagues, Jacobsen was a hero to the baseball fans in Seattle. Partly, this was because of his size and physical appearance. He was six feet four inches tall, weighed 260 pounds, had a shaved head, and sported a bright red goatee. Fans surrounded him after the games, wanting his autograph. One newspaper reporter called him a "cult figure" and another compared him to American folk heroes like Paul Bunyan. Fans wrote letters to newspapers saying he was one of the brightest spots for the future of the Seattle baseball team. Within three weeks, he was up to seven home runs. Some hits were long enough to reach into the upper decks of ballparks, as much as the length of one and a half football fields.

Then, almost as suddenly as he had started playing well, he faded. While he had seven home runs in a little more than three weeks after he arrived in the major leagues, in the next three weeks, he hit only two. His batting average fell from .320 to .275 and his slugging percentage dropped from .640 to .500.

As it turned out, he had injured his knee and tried to continue playing despite the pain. When he saw his doctor, a test showed he had torn cartilage and needed surgery. The hero's season was over. He said at the time that he thought he would be back in the major leagues the next season, but the following year, he was in the minor leagues again. Jacobsen hit poorly, perhaps because of his knee injury. For a few years, he tried to stay in baseball. He played for a season in an independent minor league team, the lowest rung of the professional ladder, and he played for a year in Mexico. In 2007, at thirty-one, an age when other major league players still have as much as a decade or more of baseball left in them, he retired. For a while he worked installing signs for a family business his father owned. Then, he found work in television as a commentator analyzing Seattle Mariners' ballgames, the team with whom he had his brief glory in 2004. He started a school for young baseball players, where he taught them how to hit as he had for a few weeks in the major leagues.

SEVEN

Caught in the Draft

In 1965, almost forty years before Jacobsen's brief time in the major leagues, a pitcher for the New York Yankees had a September very much like the few weeks that Jacobson had.

The pitcher was Rich Beck and he seemed on the verge of a successful baseball career. He was twenty-five and in his fourth season as a professional ballplayer. That season, the New York Yankees had assigned him to their double-A minor league team in Columbus, Georgia, and Beck ranked among the best hurlers in the Southern League. His thirteen victories, 2.60 earned run average (ERA), and 124 strikeouts earned him a place on the All Star team. Even more spectacular, on the last day of the season, he pitched a two-hit shutout that clinched the league title for Columbus; it was their first championship in almost twenty years.

As a reward, the Yankees promoted him to the major league team in September. Ever since he was a small boy, Beck had dreamed of pitching in the big leagues. He was so excited by the opportunity that he and his wife jumped into their car and drove the 700 miles from Georgia to New York City in a single day. After they checked into their hotel, Beck walked to Yankee Stadium to take a look at what would be his baseball home.

1965 had been a bad year for the

Yankees. Although they had won the league championship fifteen times in the previous twenty years, they would finish in sixth place out of ten teams, their worst record since 1925. Even so, as Beck reached the ballpark and stepped out of the dugout onto the field, he thought about so many of the greatest ballplayers in history who were Yankees: Babe Ruth, Lou Gehrig, Joe DiMaggio. One of the all-time greats, Mickey Mantle, was still with the Yankees, and Beck was thrilled at the thought that he would be Mantle's teammate.

Beck got into his first major league game on September 14, the starting pitcher against the then-Washington (D.C.) Senators. He pitched a terrific game, lasting seven innings, allowing only one run and striking out eight hitters. New York won 3–1.

Five days later, he was again the starting pitcher, this time against the Detroit Tigers in Yankee Stadium. The Tigers were formidable that season; two of their hitters would rank among the top three in the league in home runs. But Beck threw a shutout against them for his second major league victory.

Although he was not as effective in his third and final game that September, losing to the Indians in Cleveland, he had impressed the Yankees in his short time with them. The *New York Times* said he was a "strong prospect for a place on the starting staff for 1966," and *The Sporting News* reported that Yankees' manager Johnny Keane said that Beck figured "pretty big for us in the future."

It was not to be.

During the off-season, the U.S. Army drafted Beck. He spent almost two years in the military, working in a payroll office on a base in Texas. When the Army discharged him, Beck tried to continue his baseball career. But his time away from the sport had caused him to lose his sharpness as a pitcher. He spent two more years in the minor leagues, trying to find the control over his pitches that had made him successful before he entered the Army, but he was never able to pitch again as he had.

After the 1969 season, he decided to give up baseball. Partly, he said later, it was that he and his wife had started a family; he felt he had to provide a more secure income for them. But there was another reason. He told a writer, "I didn't want to have to feel like that, on pay day, I would have to back up to the pay window because I was embarrassed that I was collecting a check when I wasn't as effective as I could be."

While some players who had such short major league careers carry bitterness with them because they didn't last as long as others might have, Beck was happy he had just gotten to The Show, if only for two weeks.

"I was in the service with a lot of eighteen-year-old guys who went to Vietnam and never came back and so I consider myself lucky," he said. "How many times does a person get to realize their dream? I didn't get to realize it for very long, but I did get to realize it."

EIGHT

Home Run

While many of the players who reached the major leagues but could not stay had short careers because of poor luck, Doug Clarey got to the major leagues because of good luck. He only appeared in nine games and had a single hit, but that hit was the sort that boys dream about: a home run in extra innings to win a baseball game. Even better for Clarey, he hit the home run in the ballpark near his boyhood home.

Clarey was born in Los Angeles, and his father raised him to play baseball. When Clarey was two and a half, his arm was strong enough that he could throw a ball across the width of his street. When he was twelve, his family moved to San Francisco and Clarey became a fan of the Giants. He dreamed of playing baseball in Candlestick Park, where Willie Mays and Willie McCovey and Juan Marichal—all destined for the Hall of Fame—played.

As they had for Bakenhaster, scouts started following Clarey in high school, and when he graduated in 1972, the Minnesota Twins signed him to a contract. Once he reached professional baseball, however, Clarey had a difficult time as a hitter. When he was a high school senior, his batting average was .570, meaning that he safely hit nearly six out of every ten times he came to the plate. In the minor leagues he struggled as a hitter, and his batting averages were never higher than .232 in his first four years. Nevertheless, he was a good fielder as a second baseman and after the 1974 season, the St. Louis Cardinals drafted him from the Twins organization. For 1975, they assigned him to their double-A minor league team in Little Rock, Arkansas.

For the Travelers, he had the lowest batting average of his career, .206. It was, in fact, one of the lowest batting averages in the league.

Because of his slump, the Cardinals demoted Clarey for the 1976 season, back to single-A. To add to his troubles, he was not even the regular second baseman for the team, but a reserve who would probably spend more time sitting on the bench than playing in the field.

That's when Clarey found his bit of good luck that allowed him to advance to the major leagues.

In the Cardinals' second game of the season, their regular second baseman was hurt trying to turn a double play. The team needed someone to replace him for the two weeks or so it would take him to heal. St. Louis had two fielders at their top minor league team that they wanted to call up to the big club. However, both players had moved between the minor and major leagues several times, and the rules of organized baseball demanded that, if the Cardinals tried to promote them again, the men would have to "clear waivers." This allowed any other team in baseball to claim them, paying the Cardinals a small amount of money for the contract. To protect the organization, the Cardinals needed to promote a player other teams could not claim.

Clarey was that player.

When the team told him they were promoting him, Clarey was surprised. "I wasn't expecting it," he told me when I talked to him about his career. "I knew I was there just to fill a spot on the roster."

Because he had always struggled as a hitter during his years in professional baseball, Clarey thought the Cardinals probably would use him late in a game if they needed a substitute fielder for second base. He figured he would have little or no opportunity to bat.

They did use him as a pinch hitter in a game against the New York Mets two days after they called him up, but he struck out. Four days later, he got into another game in the ninth inning, as a replacement at second base.

Another four days passed and the team was in Clarey's home town, San Francisco. The dream he had as a boy came true: he was the hero who won the ballgame for his team.

After nine innings, the regulation length of a ballgame, the score was 1–1. Both teams scored another run in the fourteenth inning. In the sixteenth inning, the Cardinals managed to get a runner on base, but then, with two outs, the pitcher was due to hit. Pitchers are generally the weakest batters on a team, and the pitcher who was to bat that inning had never come to the plate in the major leagues in his career.

The Cardinals needed a pinch hitter to replace him, and the last hitter on the bench was Clarey.

On the third pitch, Clarey hit a fly ball down the left field line that barely cleared the wall for a home run. Two runs scored, and the Cardinals had the victory, 4–2.

When Clarey came into the locker room after the game, his teammates gave him a standing ovation. Nine days later, just before the Cardinals started their first game back at home after playing on the road for a week and a half, the team held a ceremony at home plate. As more than 15,000 fans watched from the stands, the Cardinals presented Clarey with an engraved watch, commemorating his home run.

Two weeks later, the team sent him back to the minor leagues. He had another opportunity later in the season, when the Cardinals' regular second baseman was injured again. Clarey spent another handful of days in the major leagues. In all that season, he batted four times, but had only the one hit, the home run.

After that year, Clarey spent two more seasons in the minor leagues but his batting average was never higher than .232. After the 1978 season, the New York Mets offered Clarey a chance to coach younger players, but Clarey, who was yet not even twenty-five, declined.

"I had just gotten married and so I didn't want to travel around the country," he said.

Clarey left baseball. For some years,

he sold commercial real estate, and today he runs a family pizza restaurant in Los Angeles.

Looking back on his career, he said, "I had a moment in the sun, which very few people ever get. It was a tremendous privilege to be able to play up there. People are impressed, men especially, because I think it's something that's in the back of their heads from the time they're a boy. No matter how good or bad a ballplayer they were, they can visualize themselves out there."

NINE

The Baseball

In the Midwest, January is not a month when most people think about baseball. Baseball is a sport for warmer days and nights. But on a weekend in the middle of the month every year, the St. Louis Cardinals hold what they call their "Winter Warm-up," a three-day event to remind fans that the season is only weeks away. In 2012, 20,000 people came to a hotel in downtown St. Louis for the Warm-up. They pushed through packed corridors and stood in long lines for the chance to meet members of the team as well as players who had retired ten, twenty, or even fifty years ago. If fans arrived early enough, they could get a seat in a meeting room to hear the general manager talk about what the team would be like that year. If they wanted, they could buy tickets that gave them the chance for a player to autograph a baseball or a photograph. Tickets for the rookie players, whom few of the fans would know, cost five dollars. For an autograph for a former player who was in the Baseball Hall of Fame or someone who had once been an All Star, a ticket could cost seventy-five or 100 dollars.

In a large room, merchants set up tables to sell souvenirs. Some displayed thousands of baseball cards. Others sold cracked baseball bats that players had used in major league games while others sold shirts and jerseys with team names enscribed on them.

One merchant offered hundreds of baseballs with player autographs. She showed most of them in small cardboard boxes, wrapped in tissue paper, or in plastic cases that protected the balls from damage. Some of the baseballs that were signed by players who had once been the best in the game cost several hundred dollars.

At one end of the table, a large cardboard box held perhaps three dozen loose, signed baseballs, each wrapped in a thin plastic sandwich bag, marked with a sticker noting the name of the player whose signature it bore. Scrawled on a flap of the box was the price for each ball inside: nine dollars, a fitting price for a baseball. Nine is the number of men in a team's lineup, and it is the number of innings in a game.

Nine dollars was less than the fifteen dollars other dealers charged for new baseballs that fans could buy so that they could ask one of the players in another room to sign them.

I stopped at the seller's display and picked through the baseballs in her box. Most were signed by players I didn't know and who, I discovered later, had never gotten to the major leagues. I did find a ball for a player whose name was familiar: Bill Ortega. I had no idea who he was or what he'd done but I gave the woman nine dollars and took the baseball home with me.

I looked up Bill Ortega. I found that he had been born in Cuba and started playing baseball as a boy. He became good enough that he eventually joined the Havana Industriales, one of the best teams in the country. With the team, Ortega earned five to ten dollars a week. According to an article I found, in 1997, when the team played in a tournament in Mexico, he told his team that he was going to take a walk to help him relax.

Instead, he went to a cemetery. In that unlikely place, he met a baseball scout from the United States who helped talented ballplayers like Ortega get to the U.S., something the Cuban government would try to prevent.

Once in the United States, Ortega played baseball in a tryout for several major league teams. The Cardinals offered him a $200,000 bonus to sign a professional contract with them.

Although he struggled in his first two years in the minor leagues and didn't hit well, the Cardinals still thought he had the ability to play major league baseball. They kept promoting him to higher levels in the minor leagues. In 1999 and 2000, he gave evidence that they were correct as he ranked among the ten best hitters in his league and made the All Star team.

Finally, in September 2001, the Cardinals moved him to the major leagues. He spent three weeks with the team that month, appeared in five games, and had five times at bat. On September 24, he hit a single with two outs in a game the Cardinals were already losing 9–3. The next batter grounded out, however, and so Ortega's hit had no significant outcome in the game or the season. Four days later, he had his last time at bat in a major league game and struck out.

Two months later, *The Sporting News* reported that Ortega might have a chance to be back with the Cardinals for the 2002 season as a reserve player. If the report was correct, he would spend most of the season on the bench, waiting to get into a game. Nevertheless, he would be in the major leagues.

It didn't happen.

Although he hit well in spring training before the 2002 season, the Cardinals sent him back to the minor leagues for the year. Before the 2003 season, the team released him. While he tried to connect with other organizations, he never played another professional game.

So, the sum of his career as a major league player was five times at bat. Most regular players—the ones who are good enough to be in the starting lineup—have five times at bat in a typical game.

Despite the spare statistics that summarized his time as a major league batter, he had been there. For three weeks, he had put on a major league uniform with the number 28 and his name spelled out on the back of the jersey. He had sat on a bench with players who were All Stars and who would, in years to follow, win awards for hitting and fielding.

Although he had done little himself during his time in the game, someone had once thought enough of him as a ballplayer to ask him to scrawl his name on a baseball. More than ten years after his brief time in the major leagues, I would find that baseball in a box on a table in a large crowded room filled with fans looking for souvenirs in the middle of winter.

I would pay nine dollars and take the baseball home and put it on a shelf with baseballs signed by greats.

There the ball still sits, evidence that Bill Ortega may have only been in the major leagues for three weeks, but he had his season in the sun.